A KINGDOM OF LOVE

Rachel Mann is an Anglican parish priest and writer. She was Poet-in-Residence at Manchester Cathedral between 2009 and 2017 and is the author of five books, including *Fierce Imaginings: The Great War, Ritual, Memory and God* (DLT, 2017). She is Visiting Fellow in Creative Writing and English at Manchester Metropolitan University. Her poetry was anthologised in Carcanet's *New Poetries VII* (2018).

A KINGDOM
OF LOVE

RACHEL MANN

CARCANET

First published in Great Britain in 2019 by
Carcanet
Alliance House, 30 Cross Street
Manchester M2 7AQ
www.carcanet.co.uk

A CIP catalogue record for this book is
available from the British Library.
ISBN 978 1 78410 857 1

Book design by Andrew Latimer
Printed in Great Britain by SRP Ltd, Exeter, Devon

The publisher acknowledges financial
assistance from Arts Council England.

Contents

III. A LESSON IN EVOLUTION

I.

A KINGDOM OF LOVE

'There's blood between us, love, my love.'
Christina Rossetti

'A poet's words can pierce us.'
Ludwig Wittgenstein

A KINGDOM OF LOVE

I return from the garden of remembrance,
I wash the dead from my hands,
I sing the versicles for Evensong, *O Lord*,
My larynx trembles with mucus and awe.

COLLECT FOR PURITY

I try to form prayer's capital word
On my tongue. O sweet imagination
Give it shape enough! *Love!*

Love should taste of something,
The sea, I think, brined and unsteady,
Of scale and deep and all we crawled out from.

Of first day, the Spirit's début,
The frantic dove torn apart,
Her feathers ash on Eden.

Yet of that which we cannot speak
We must pass over in silence –
Selah!

The Spirit itself maketh intercession for us
With groanings
Which cannot be uttered.

FIDES QUAERENS

Am I required to believe
In the uncorruption of saints,
The Mother's timeless womb?

There is limit, even if limit
Is never drawn. (I cannot
Give an instance of every rule.)

I don't know what 'believe in' means
In the vast majority of cases,
Which is to say I think it enough

To acknowledge glamour of words –
Relic, body, bone – I think
Mystery is laid in syllables, syntax,

Miracle a kind of grammar,
Milk to train the tongue.

UBI CARITAS

We learn the world, the first world
Of love and drool and sweet milk
Through lips.

What surprise that prayer shares
A language with kisses?

THE ORDINAL

I've lived for the feelings of others,
That's a listening of sorts,

What have I learnt? That self
Is bitumen, black as tar,

Oh, how slowly we flow, oh
How slowly we flow, we crack with age.

I've lived for the feelings of others,
A philosophy of sorts. I've heard

Self give up its final word,
Coughs and whispers in

Hospitals and nursing homes.
Oh, how slowly we flow, oh.

Before holy or righteous, before the Law,
Before sound was distilled (so many crossings-out)
Into *bet, aleph, niqqud*, before all that: Song.

Oh, to taste fricatives – damp from lip and palate –
Dental trills, the Spirit chewed by teeth,
Ejected from lungs, an offering.

Oh, to know before, before, before the Book: Decision.
Should the Fruit be plucked or crushed?
And, love, what place love?

EXTREME UNCTION

I've anointed the dying, smeared oil
On the book of human skin,
I've seen what we're written in –
Creases, scars, scabs –
Witnessed terminal breath,

I've known the final room;
Christ lies, brittle on a hospital bed,
Something slips free, a syllable of self –
Sweet trill. Deep, deep the sound goes –
He sings of Cross and ash,

Soon, it will be accomplished,
He dreams of milk and drool,
Of bitter birth, brush of prayer on lips –
He dreams of mother's kiss, secret love –
My God, why have you forgotten me?

COMPLINE

Why should I not have lovers too?
Which is to say, when no one else
Comes near, God will have to do.

Prayer is the body's work, *is*,
I was taught to steeple my fingers
As a child, form a spire, *Like this!*

Prayer ascends, it is naked, *shiver.*
O God, avert thine eyes! Thine eyes
Are multitude, thy tongue is bitter.

CREDO

I am wracked by assertions:
God is *not* a name,
God is Love, God is, God *is*.

A person without a name is not,
That is one of history's truths
(I have seen the films of the camps

Where names are erased).
If God, if if if, if God
Is to be claimed as lover

I must multiply names:
Pneuma, The Three-in-One,
Mother, Tetragrammaton,

Al-Wajid, Bhagavan, Diabolos,
Jesus, Jesus puts a tongue
Into my mouth, I Am.

A KINGDOM OF LOVE (2)

If the world is all that is the case,
If it is the totality of facts, not of things,
What then of prayer?

I sit in church, say authorised words,
The Lord almighty grant us a quiet night
And a perfect end. Amen.

Say them out loud though I'm alone.
That is how it is at this hour,
I make my singular witness

Offer the fact of prayer – a formula,
And more: the compromise of centuries
Made *valid*.

What matter is it if there is no god
To validate? The conditions lack,
Prayer's a game and a fine one,

Our help is in the name of the Lord. Selah!
Night after night, words lock into place,
A game without novelty.

There is no reference point,
No object grounding it,
Beyond anticipated Love.

GLORIA

I.

At Mattins, I say authorised words,
O Lord, open thou my lips,
And my mouth shall proclaim thy praise.

Say them out loud,
This uttering by rule a glory of mouth:
Love as call, a bird desperately sings

Your black-dust words
From a city tree:
Eli, Eli, lema Sabachthani,

O glorious hour of need!
A mating cry, the last, the last
Departure, exile, world.

II.

Accept my body as transgression,
My lungs for greed, guts for sloth,
My bones for pride, and envy: my loins.

Receive my tongue with all its
Honeyed compromise; there will be tears.
My skin: confessional, a slate cleaned.

III.

Sin is hymnal,
Body's original psalm,
It is love-chorale,

Never forget, never,
Rome used criminals as victims
In feasts – as Icarus

Thrown from a roof,
Dismembered as Orpheus,
Castrated as Attis.

Imagine! Mouth, skin, bone.
To sing such sweet mar,
Broken, such sin.

IV.
I kneel at communion rail,
And I might believe light can be sour,
The moon red, that I kneel

At world's rim, a herald;
I might believe in Return,
His discalced step sensitive as a fox's,

A tap and scratch on stone,
His scent, pelt and forest,
That this is what new creation

Smells like, an unlearning of words.

CATECHESIS

In college we learnt
Morning and evening star are not the same,
'Meaning' different from 'reference';

Thus, he who fell could be Venus,
His magnificence so bright
It challenged the utter uniform of dawn,

Lucifer, a point of flame
Plunges earthward, black comet,
Enough to draw crowds to point and gasp,

To ask the question we ask
When nature (faith?) abandons its course:
What private prospect dies in this display?

THE APOCALYPSE OF JOHN

I.

We gather at church door
For a body, and perhaps
This is creak of Last Day,

Ten of us, eyes downcast,
Behold! A universe in pavement cracks;

I hold a Word in my hands – *Eleison* –
I whisper, *In God, nothing is ever truly lost,*
But already a Seal

Is broken and I am sick
Of rain and storm, and pale horse,

And pale horse comes to my door
And perhaps this is Last Day,
And rain, and rain, and angels

Silent in Heaven, and dare I believe,
In God, nothing is ever truly lost?

II.

A body dies and I sing Requiem,
Man hath but a short time to live,
Man hath but the validity of material things!

Requiem is black universe,
Word is gravity,
Body is praise!

III.

Yet to find one's final form,
Surely that's the meaning

Of *spes contra spem*?
The ashes of a neighbour wait

In my study for burial in a garden
Of grit and peonies and loam,

Soon to be carried a final time,
Soon to be earthbound,

A statement in ontology.
Ecstatic. Cool. Unravelled.

CORPUS CHRISTI

I.

Body crumbles into its appointed place,
Two foot by two, powder swirls above hole's lip;
I sing my words, *ashes to ashes, dust to dust*,
We are people of unclean hands,

As I pour damp afternoon into Sheol,
My skin dark with soil and burnt bone;
Take me with you, the dim day responds,
Take me, priest; we understand each other, let us thrive.

II.

Body crumbles into its appointed place,
I survey *Life Everlasting* from grave's lip,
Witness flesh give consent to earth's forgiveness,
A ministration of worms and *Death No More*.

I scrape from the tub the last of self's
Gritted truth and walk off,
Sure of nothing except soil and winter,
That our end is a wreckage of heaven.

A KINGDOM OF LOVE (3)

If, in the Resurrection, I shall be raised
To congregation – face-to-face,
All eyeless skulls, so much dust

Ached with near-forgotten form
(a finger, teeth, tongue) – if so,
I shall know only you.

All else, washed-clean,
Virgin robes,
Metaphor for the begin-again.

If I am raised, I shall not care if you
Will be like unto severed hand
(Forgetful, free) and I the stump, mourning;

And if, on that day, poetry shall be done
With its need of hearts,
I too shall walk glory-bound,

A Kingdom of Love, I shall
Sing other songs –
Separate and singular, Joy.

II.

MYTHOLOGIES

'All the great things have been denied…'
Wallace Stevens

'Myth is neither a lie nor a confession: it is an inflexion.'
Roland Barthes

CHAUCER ON ECCLES NEW ROAD

'Canterbury Gardens comprises a hundred stylish apartments
for the modern city-dweller…' – Estate Agent's Leaflet

From between the lines – yellow, white, stained –
speak, Theseus, speak. Of the great chain of love,
kyndely enclyning. Breathe and speak, worthy knyght.

Requite, dronke Robyn, or *stynt thy clappe*.
Traffic has a language of its own:
whispers and sighs, chime of speeding steel,

and prying's no sin. Inquire of tram tracks,
of *Goddes pryvetee*, how long it takes to lay.
Gras tyme is doon, my fodder is now forage,

A plea for peace, Oswald reve, but here's truth:
Til we be roten, kan we nat be rype.
We all become earth, but mortar and brick?

The Pardoner is a court, prefab walls,
Ycrammed ful of cloutes and of bones,
carpet and paint. Shopping malls are relics

swarmed with pilgrims. Your garden, Theseus,
is poison. Enclyne your roof, shelter me.
Til it be roten in mullok or in stree.

READING OVID ON THE UNDERGROUND

Look, Niobe comes... as beautiful as anger will let her be.

Mansion House, Monument, Cannon Street, Bank,
the electric underworld: carriages of wrists,
elbows, ripe armpits. *Stand clear of the doors.*
Words curve on all the walls. *Last chance to see!*
*****, *A Triumph!* Pin-up faces peel.
Lear stares, his girls. He waits our flattery.

No phases of the moon for us. No sun
to mark the days. It's all show: white light, glare.
At the edge of electrocution
corpse boys, corpse girls walk the tunnels
and halls: stale breath, bodies out of time,
they teach me the meaning of words:

frantic, fears, daughters, sons, tears, alone, gone.
St Pancras, Angel, Old Street, Moorgate. Bank.
St Pancras, do you ever hear our prayers?
Our prayers are escalators. *Scala*
sounds so classy, *elevating,* but handrails
are loops of black. Vinyl prayers spin on.

Covent Garden, Piccadilly, Leicester Square.
As far down as this world goes, I go down.
Staircases move up, topple out of sight,
metal waterfalls, but no one believes my tears.
It's theatre-land. Everyone a busker here.
Michelle, ma belle. Dry your tears, I seh.

East. East. All gods arise in the east.
East Acton. East Finchley. East Cote. East Ham.
Back to the source, through the burial grounds
the Navvies bored, back beyond the dead.
Heaven's the top of a stair.
Hell's a blur, hot wind, an empty platform.

Mamucium: breast-place, mother, Eve –
Oh bone of my flesh, flesh of my bone,
Clay and water dredged, sweet Daub Hole.

Tonight the mysteries of glaciers
Spend themselves on tarmac. Ice-caps soak us.
We're the damp-arsed. Your favoured kids.

So this is what it's like to be cast out –
East of Eden, East of Salford, benched
With drunks. Beyond the wall, buses squeal.

We're in the dark and forget the garden
Was an asylum once. Bright lights, fierce crowds
Dance along its edge. We'd leave if we could.

Mamucium: breast-place, mother, Eve –
Clay and water. Raw bone. It's what we are.
Can you hear me, Eve? Our breath is fumes.

ST ELISABETH ZACHARIAS

Come. Beyond thirst, beyond tending,
where rose petals crisp, water greens
in a vase.

Move closer. Breathe my dust, my very flesh
settling. Be dust with me. Here where
we place the things we've gathered –

the china labradors,
the endless cats,
the *Cliff Richard* plates.

Isn't this how it should be? Piling
fold on fold, letting gravity pull
on our bones, till we can resist no more?

Don't touch me. My cells ache. My skin
so thin spiders fall through.
It would be a sin to hold someone else.

South of Stoke, England in the snow,
Only time I think it safe to speak of love
Of country; when coverage is incomplete,

Green breaks through white, green, green:
Youth, promise, *Songs of Innocence*,
A steel windmill spins, and trees are bones.

I could believe in silence beyond window-glass,
That's snow for you, I adore its clichés,
Oh, white vacuum reach inside.

Let me take my chance, speak of love
Of country while no one can hear or breathe –
Passengers pass along the aisle,

An attendant pours tea, hands me bacon
In a roll. South, south, deeper into territory,
'*This is England*', who can spot my fakery?

My announcements – tannoy-bright –
'*Here, Arthur Badon stormed, Grail lost,
Rejoice! Boudicca, Gawain, Lud*',

My pronouncements: facsimiles (of what?);
Snow becomes complete – whiteout, England,
Whiteout, England. England.

ACHILLES IN ALBION

We know so little, Patroclus, about praise,
You and I, who taste sour limit of skin,
Pitch and roll, pitch and roll in troopships,

About praise! Praise, Patroclus, avoids rain,
Climate is truth, sick fact, grey on grey;
Whale-road smashes into chalk,

Our beachhead crumbles, I found relics
In the night attack: Brittle stars and snake stones,
Did they ever know praise? Our enemy lurks

In glass towers, I see glow, backlights,
People transact, tap, tap, tap, zeros and ones,
Tap, tap, tap. Near-praise. Not near enough.

A BRIEF HISTORY OF ANGLICANISM

I.
Suppose. Suppose prayer
Is a spark thrown

On a wall, a shadow;
Suppose it's fire,

Though flame is surely
Spent metaphor;

We lay the trap
In candle and stone,[1]

For Him who delights in light,
We say:

He shows His wings, yes,
Perhaps he shows His wings.

II.
Suppose there is no secret after all,[2]
The centuries of stone and Table,
High chorale of boys,
Bishop and priest,

All the lines of doctrine,
The aching knees (oh, the aching knees)
Even the work of Him for whom we gather,
And the Mother, *O Blessèd Mother,*

No more than arrangements
Of rumour, misapprehension
For spectacle's sake;
As if the absence of His body

As if the excitement of disciples
Were sufficient
For toil and chant and festival,
A pageant of secrets, a veil, a cloak.[3]

III.
Oh, that my words were now written!
Oh, that they were printed in a book!
That they were graven with an iron pen
And lead, for ever in the rock![4]

1   R.S. Thomas, 'The Empty Church', l. 1.
2   Christina Rossetti, 'Winter: My Secret', l. 8.
3   Ibid, l. 12.
4   The Book of Job, 19: 23–25.

LEX ORANDI

A slow train, I'm carried north to speak
Of mystery, *out* and *in*, *The Divine Vision*.

Windows jolt and I see fields north
Of Northallerton, ridges grassed over,

Echo of strip farmers, so meagre,
Long lines of soil the difference

Between life and death. Further out,
Steam plumes where horizon should be,

That is what electricity looks like
After it's passed on; finally, Durham,

Cathedral towers wrapped in white
(Swaddling? bandages?)

So this is glory, glory-bound,
I might close my eyes or pull down

The blind, but why should I?
It's the inner eye that sees,

My carriage companions stare
At table tops, computer screens,

The man opposite mutters,
A Love Supreme, A Love Supreme,

His voice raw winter, a cold rain falls.
He knows, he knows what I do not.

Somewhere beneath the dry blast of sun:
Jones. D, David, Dai, Jonah –
Nineveh's boy-prophet.

In his pack, hard tack and stencils, the loneliness
Of words, vials of the Blood,
And haunch of Holy Lamb –

Behold, he comes, Jonah-bach,
Behold, reluctantly, to engrave a century –
Cry out, saith the Lord.

Out of the belly of Sheol, he draws spitsticker
And scorper, dead men ever-near,
He draws out sharpening-stone,

He cuts wounds in wood,
He sings: dead men feel no fear, dead men,
Their greatcoats hold promises deep –

He too has needs: of sleep, of dreams,
Of Pellam, the Lady of the Pool, his tools
Carve: *Repent of thy wickedness. Begin!*

PILGRIMS AT LUKE COPSE

'I was a dreamer ever...' – Ivor Gurney

Azure electric, an unbroken sky above Serre,
though a hint of cumulus, a curd summit
for the church's spire. We've come to measure

the distance between here and there, past and now,
from wood to village, time as geography –
days measured in inches, months in yards gained,

a decade in how long it took to plot the remains,
the ploughman surveys the field's chalk and bone
harvest. *They buried them where they fell,*

the guidebook says, gravestones bring other news:
Lest we and *Greater Love, Nobly, Willingly,*
To the Memory, To the Glory and *Pace, Pace, Pace*

while Portland white bleeds green, the windward edge
enough to take bearings, discern the direction
of winter and storm, the yet to come.

Till then, sleepers, dream ever. A cornfield
at Ampney Crucis as May turns gold, green shoots
quickens to the swallows' dance. It might be England.

TO A WATER GOD

I want to trace you back through the line of a river,
Out from the end-point: brown waves, engine grease,
Vast elsewhere. I want to touch your sores:
Docks and rotting wharfs, cranes flaked to rust,

I want you on my palms. Further back,
When you zig-zagged, young and pissed,
Jumped off cliffs, back and back to birth,
Your first day – to touch your pristine word.

CHRISTENING

O unquiet Sunday! Behold:
Pews, scratchy suits, so much tan,

Fake, fake, an infant mewls his prayer.
I offer my refrain: *Out of bondage,*

Children of Israel, Out of Egypt,
To promised lands. I pour liquid

Into bowl of stone: *Be buried, Christ;*
Spirit, wash us in thy rivers clean.

I pour troublous waters, Deep –
Here migrant boats crash,

Dreams drown green, sea plucks shore, ·
Empty, empty, empty.

Was it thus when He took His turn
At Jordan, 'Baptist, suffer it to be so'?

So, mewl, child, mewl, we fall and drown.
There are rivers to be crossed,

Deep – *In name*
Of Father, Son and Holy Ghost.

DRESS

after Sharon Olds

Heart red, cut-knee red,
made from perle cotton, the lustre of sunset on a lake.
But not for showing off:
not a take me out, let stars fall from the sky,
firecracker kind of dress;
just a dress for an eight-year-old girl,
a simple pinafore to be worn on boring Saturdays
watching TV, drowsy from the scent of baking
seeping under the kitchen door.
A small flower near the hem, perhaps,
a daisy stitched in by mum,
something to pick at, fray, one day dig out.
A dress maybe never even worn, hanging
in the wardrobe, occasionally touched,
smiled upon. To simply have known it was mine
in those days. To have had something.

The Brothers provide me with a book –
Not expected language of Grace and Love
Hidden in a drawer, but another:
The Lure of Faraway Places by Angelo Costalonga,
'*Hotelplan International Award winner (1985)*
For best photographic book.'

Enlighten me, Angelo, bright messenger,
Be my Virgil, no, only Beatrice will do;
I am ready, receive me as you received the monk
In your cover-shot: with wide-angled grace,
May I too stand beneath Sacred Fig, mountain ablaze
With cloud. Enlighten me.

I want to be trusted with full palette, but not yet;
Keep from me silver and crimson forest,
Keep from me emerald-eyed woman, she smiles,
Holds up gift of frog – *just a little higher*
I want to see the gold of its eyes –
Keep from me river of lilies and turmeric.

Grant me technicolour, but not yet. First, words:
'A profession of faith does not mean weakness',
'Will desperation or hope break out?',
'In the realm of intuition concepts are encumbrance',
Tell me, Angelo, how you have heard it said,
'It is easy for Bangladeshis to be happy';

Angelo, Virgil, Beatrice – you and I know
Lust of Eye is downfall of many a Vow,
I study your book, World without End,
And new wine burns through my skin;
I, too, feel desire to wear islands as a necklace. Angelo,
Have you come to tempt or betray? Show up my sin.

BOOK OF EZEKIEL

I.

City! City of God, Salem, *selah!*
Heaven's cast-off, stained with spite and oil,
Oh, shining damp cobble land, breathe.

Come Ancoats, old clogger,
Senile suburb, come. Recall
Beehive, Phoenix, drysalters on Stony Brow,

Fume with coal and shale.
You make all things new, tarted mills sing,
But Salem, old friend, we dream,

We wear rain for gladness and tears.
Miracle us, thou Storms of Baptism,
Wash away our glass-clad shame.

II.

Pure throat. That's how a city sings after birds:
Basso profundo, jug-jug-juggernaut, listen
If ye have ears to hear –

Cough, ye children of tar, cough,
Somewhere a two-stroke, bad soprano, sings,
'How high must we rise to live?'

III.

Pray for me, Padre. Salem leans close,
Old diesel lungs, *Pray for me.*

A quid pro quo, I say, teach me
Your names – ninety-nine and more,

YHWH, Jehovah-shammeh, Mocha Parade –
Unpronounceables, sweet street names.

Decision grows dirty so quickly,
Pray for me, Padre, Oh, pray for me in return,

I'll spare you change, witness your names,
YHWH, Jehovah-shammeh, Mocha Parade;

See, I am conjuror. Love erases doubt,
Can be measured in silver coin.

FALLEN

after Michael Symmons Roberts

You tumbled into the dark and I held you,
awkward as a foal, a confusion of feet and hands,
demanding cigarettes and whisky.

I marvelled at the flakes of ice,
black as old snow, falling from your skin,
the crackle as you entered my bed.

At night I'd try to learn you,
map your shoulders and neck,
the planes of your chest, the stumps on your back.

I fed you roast lamb, figs, food with weight.
Asked you the only question. *Can you ever go back?*
Held a finger to your lips when you began to speak.

PERSEPHONE ON KINGSWAY

'It seems that Persephone's only sin
was to reach out to pluck a narcissus' – Luce Irigaray

I.

All along the long miles, bloom:
All along, stems shake out gold,
In Arcady I called them jonquil,

Daffs (if you must), all along
Didsbury, Burnage, Levenshulme,
Signs sing: *Dual Carriageway, Children!*

Slow Down, Slow Down!
Spring leaks from my toes,
I have prayer, honeyed, sweet:

May every day be blue electric,
May every day cast blossom far and wide,
Further than Hades from heaven;

My skin is vitamin, I am root, quickened.
Roads break, greyscale shines.

II.

All along, stems shake out gold,
All along the long miles, they cram
Central reservation, swaying fire –

I could almost reach, pluck, but
Cars, vans, thousands, they fume.
All along the long miles

Artics, thousands, Eddie Stobart,
Their names: *Ann-Marie*, *Sophie-Kate*,
Mary-Jane, never, never mine;

Health is so near to sickness,
Carriageway is poison, flowers fade.
He is close, a question:

Is it better to step into road, make it quick,
Or, tantalise, make everyone wait?

JOSEPH AND THE ANGEL

In a room, perhaps. Saw and bench,
plane and chisel, the tools of the trade.

But – to his delight – a boy again,
trees still to be climbed,

not yet caring what's a mattock, what's a yoke,
opening a window, just to let the bright elsewhere in.

All this time, the visitor's words,
insistent, the hum of bees brought indoors,

one question again and again:
Do you understand?

Knowing he should speak,
marvelling at the cleanliness

of his new-made hands.

QUI HABET AURES

Above, fighter-jet, white line in blue,
I hear boom, break-through, mark
In a barrier of sound. So, this is Retreat –

Prayer and intercession, centuries
Of martyrs and saints – let there be thunder,
Soon rain. And if I'm yet to retreat

Far enough to hear St Cecilia pray,
I walk dunes, song brushes my ears,
Blackbird perhaps, thrush or lark

Sending news of yet-to-come;
Further in, tinnitus reaches for top C,
My head a room with secret frequencies,

Perhaps this is how Kingdom sounds.
Out in the bay, eighty thousand tonnes
Heads for dock – treasures and goods,

Within its mist-shroud, riches of nations.
Further out: windmills, a forest of white,
They spin, I barely see, I cannot hear.

BOOK OF JOB

I.

Suffer the little children, saith the Lord,
Suffer, come unto me.
Blur of bodies, black, blue, red,

They who sit, sit only temporarily,
Stop, move, in, out, in, out;

Though time enough for lovers, just enough,
They hold and breathe, press skin-to-skin,
Such tight lips:

Not our last goodbye, not
Our last goodbye, not yet, my sweet,

Message me. Vast digital boards blaze,
Sheffield, Stockport, Staines,
So many destinations,

Is this Europe? Wartime?
Bags dragged, whole lives.

II.

I wish I were a reader of books,
Dante, Milton, I would have quotes.

Instead: Burgers, chicken, boxes, pints,
Coffee. So many suck
On straws, mmm heavenly,

Suck, move, look, suck, look
At screens. Surely soon there must

Be news, Gospel. Announcements,
Alterations, platforms, news –
Just enough, news of somewhere,

Hades perhaps. A boatman,
His oar beats the reluctant across, across.

PAROUSIA

'This train is bound for glory' – Traditional

We leave the station and world grows small,
Spires and steeples hold their own
With terraces, Aldi, Asda, so many carparks,

Prominence changes. Do I grow smaller too?
Out from skyscraped earth, I am still clay,
I am clay and glass,

Evidence beyond doubt: finger strokes screen,
Such lust, such habit, my hands
Know what I love;

A song of Byrd's plays, my phone sings
Diliges Dominum, sixteenth-century
Draws close:

Thou shalt love, love thy God with all
Heart, Soul, with all Mind.
Thou shalt love neighbour as thyself.

III.
A LESSON IN EVOLUTION

'God created a number of possibilities...'
Graham Greene

THE RISEN LIFE

You wake to sting between shoulder blades
as if someone's folded a crease down your back,
silence hurts, and the light unexpected –
grey, not quite morning, glowing at the edges

as if electric is involved. So many people,
lying down, confined, each in their own bay,
slow heave of chests, a faint scent
(antiseptic perhaps?), the calm.

Not remembering for a second what has happened to you,
then feeling out from the inside a kind of shock
shivering down through your forehead, teeth, neck,
a fear about what might have been removed.

There is a nurse, she could be a nurse, someone who smiles,
who is not afraid of wounds, whose eyes twinkle
as she holds a finger to her mouth
when you start to speak.

AWAKE AT THREE A.M. WHAT IS KNOWN:

that somewhere else,
in Anadyr or Kamchatka, say,
a man is organising his regrets into a song,
searching down through the arpeggios
for a proper place to start.

Further out still,
a wolf howls its own heartbreak,
by a lake, a shivering child skims stones.

GIVE IT A NAME

the nurse says, pulling off the bag.
'*It helps.*'

Well, why not, then?
It was good enough for explorers,
thrusting flags into virgin land.
For Adam too.

But this is something else:
new lips cut in my abdomen,
stoma, meaning *mouth.*

So, go on. Speak.
Fumble with vowel sounds,
stutter over nouns. Name yourself.

'*Do try,*' the nurse says.
'*Jagger,*' I suggest.

A LESSON IN EVOLUTION

The specialist wants to try seaweed,
feed it strand by strand into the cavern
below, leave it to settle in pools,
do its work among the creatures
they left behind.

Who knew a body was so much sea?
That beneath the crust of skin,
there are trenches where beasts
angle for prey, spark light
from nothing but themselves.

All life was water once.
Perhaps I'll travel home,
relearn the trick of gills, fin and scale.
Retreat from mud.
Thirty leagues out, silver-eyed, free at last.

HIGH DEPENDENCY

We are where
miracles hide in curtain folds
where breath is regulated

bodies drift and halt
work according to plans we do not understand
dispensing dreams

veins of red and black rise from our arms
plastic coils extend out and upwards searching
grace falls with leisure of snow

NOMENCLATURE

If Our Lady Amherst has Man of Noon,
And Julian, her Sister Wound,
I too beg a name for Name;

I should like secret –
Whispered behind my hand,
I should like confidence (with whom?);

To have words for Word –
How might they feel on my tongue?
Should I prefer my mouth scraped to blood,

A potsherd on my lips,
Might I be soothed, honey and milk,
His Love?

Word, Name, wait for me,
Wait, till I am sealed, in Cell, or Room,
My room, my own white room,

My body robed for dreams.
Wait till inner life is enough,
Till my skin – lined, creased – retreats.

VESPERS

'Lord, now lettest thou thy servant depart in peace...'

I.
Half light, eventide, spill your shadows now,
Soften rush of day, sooth me in the gloom.

Half light, flare and burn, hold back night,
Spark and fizz, gutter me, reveal what remains.

II.
Some evenings it is enough to stand and breathe,
To wait outside Chapel, receive chime of bells.

Hands pull and release their cords,
And none need understand, not me, no more

Than trees at yard's edge or the dead
Untroubled in their tombs, earth unmoved.

III.
Imagined Love. Day by day
I remember its founding form:
A man at supper with friends,
The night before he died, etc.

'Re-member,' theologians say.
Too clever, I think, this attempt
To make the holy whole,
Reverse the violation.

A priest's business is sacrifice,
The people approach with open hands,
I bear bread and shame, we say *Amen*.
We know many things without proof.

COMPLINE

Night, and my offering is due,
I have electronics, touch screens, apps,
My stall is cold, a candle casts white flush

Of death across my hands;
Sacrifice, the ever-sacrifice – Table,
Bread, Wine, flesh, flesh, flesh –

Awaits, deeper in the dark,
Further away than ever before,
O God make speed to save us.

My knees crack on stone, oh prayer,
Holy Ghost! Come! If, and if all things,
Defend us from perils, dangers of night.

I search whitewashed walls for glimpse –
Flick of feather, magic-light, dove –
I look down. Backlit icons await my grasp.

LAUDS

'I only ask a Tune at Midnight' – Emily Dickinson

The gatehouse locks, and night,
I mark hours in chimes,
And heat, heat makes its prayer –

A slow refrain, stifling. Brick
And wood store warmth so deep,
And I write, look across Close,

Called by chimes toward Cathedral,
It's out there, stone and scaffold,
If only I could see buttresses fly;

Do penitents still shuffle
On their knees, does anyone
Carry His corpus through streets?

No light, only bells, chime, chime,
And Owl, counterpoint,
Its hoot an open window on mine.

Dare I sing of saints and martyrs
Stained in glass, of our Lord
(Cornerstone torn), of Cathedral?

Sister Owl sings, an open window,
And Spire soars, Heaven,
And soon light, demon-dawn.

MATTINS

Beyond windows, a chorus,
Bright alto, a thousand hidden lungs

And throats – furious love;
Dawn at the Abbey

And I am wide awake.
Wide: a river, a canyon, an ocean.

A soul? Risk is God's way –
Frail Babe, Nails and Cross, a Garden –

So why not? Song crowds my bed,
I cannot sleep, chatter, chatter;

Perhaps there is only hymnal
And end of winter, and psalm –

Charms of finches, herd of wrens,
Blackbird, robin, thrush,

Beyond windows, surely trees,
Stripped and boned, perhaps

They'll wake, spit out shoots,
Perhaps, I'll draw up blinds.

EVENSONG

*'Love is a phoenix that will revive
its own ashes'* – Thomas Traherne

September, and the orchard sags with prayer:
Strip the Fruit of Sin! Reap! Reap!

Wye lifts lime, spins pools of silt at the tip
Of fields and it is late, late, late, oh priest

Hurry on! Sing, O miserable offender,
Within thy walls of stone. Hurry on,

Witness His truth:
Glory is not a word, God is, God is

Neither noun nor verb, but shears laden fields,
He reapeth where he doth not sow.

ACKNOWLEDGEMENTS

Thanks are due to the editors of the following publications, in which some of these poems previously appeared: *Agenda, Beautiful Dragons, New Poetries VII* (Carcanet 2018), *The North, PN Review, Theology, Under the Radar* and the *Hippocrates Prize for Poetry and Medicine.*